10/13

Makerspaces

by Samantha Roslund and
Emily Puckett Rodgers

CHERRY LAKE PUBLISHING • ANN ARBOR, MICHIGAN

CHERRY LAKE Publishing

A Note to Adults: Please review the instructions for the activities in this book before allowing children to do them. Be sure to help them with any activities you do not think they can safely complete on their own.

A Note to Kids: Be sure to ask an adult for help with these activities when you need it. Always put your safety first!

Published in the United States of America by Cherry Lake Publishing
Ann Arbor, Michigan
www.cherrylakepublishing.com

Series Editor: Kristin Fontichiaro
Photo Credits: Cover and page 1, ©SparkFunElectronics/www.flickr.com/ CC-BY-2.0; pages 4, 6, and 9, ©plural/www.flickr.com/CC-BY-SA-2.0; page 5, ©maltman23/www.flickr.com/CC-BY-SA-2.0; page 7, ©jam232/ www.flickr.com/CC-BY-2.0; page 13, ©theycallmebrant/www.flickr.com/ CC-BY-SA-2.0; page 16, ©Hannu-Makarainen/www.flickr.com/CC-BY-SA-2.0; page 17, courtesy of Michigan Makers; pages 19 and 29, ©steevithak/ www.flickr.com/CC-BY-SA-2.0; pages 20 and 27, ©Fort Meade/www.flickr.com/ CC-BY-2.0; page 23, ©jaaron/www.flickr.com/CC-BY-2.0; page 24, ©Elvert Barnes/www.flickr.com/CC-BY-2.0

Cataloging-in-Publication data is available from the Library of Congress
Roslund, Samantha.
  Makerspaces and hackerspaces/by Samantha Roslund and Emily Puckett Rodgers.
      pages cm.—(Makers as innovators)
  Includes bibliographical references and index.
  ISBN 978-1-62431-141-3 (lib. bdg.)—ISBN 978-1-62431-207-6 (e-book)—
ISBN 978-1-62431-273-1 (pbk.)
  1. Social networks—Juvenile literature. 2. Do-it-yourself work—Juvenile literature.
3. Workshops—Juvenile literature. I. Rodgers, Emily Puckett. II. Title.
  HM741.R67 2014
  302.3—dc23   2013007053

Cherry Lake Publishing would like to acknowledge the work of The Partnership for 21st Century Skills. Please visit www.p21.org for more information.

Printed in the United States of America
Corporate Graphics Inc.
July 2013
CLFA13

Contents

Chapter 1

What Are Makers?

Have you ever sat down at your kitchen table and pulled out paper, glue, wood, or other supplies to work on a project? But then, right when you get started, your mom tells you that dinner's almost ready and you need to pack everything up? Have you ever

Do you like to build or invent things? You might be a maker!

Makers use a variety of tools and supplies to complete their projects.

wanted to make wood shelves to display your favorite items, but your family doesn't own power tools? Have you ever worked alone on a project but wished someone were there to help you figure out the toughest steps? If any of these things has happened to you, then you might be a maker without a space.

Today's makers use advanced technology such as 3D printers to make their ideas come to life.

Makers are people who do things to improve the world around them. If something is broken, they try to fix it. They try to find solutions to problems. Someone who likes to build new things or use tools or materials in new ways can be considered a maker. Anyone who has ever had an idea for a new invention and then made that idea a reality is a maker. Makers love to create, tinker, and play with the world and the resources around them. They also love to share their experiences with others. This is how a maker group gets started.

Think about life a hundred years ago. Almost every item was made one at a time, mostly by hand. Things were customized to fit an individual person's needs. Chairs were made just the right size for the people who would sit in them, and clothes were cut and sewn to fit their wearers. Today, most everyday items are built in factories, but the desire to make stuff by hand hasn't gone away. Now, makers continue the long tradition of tinkering with, changing, and improving their inventions as well as things made by others.

All wooden items were once created by hand.

Some makers and inventors throughout history have worked alone. And there are makers who do—and have done—incredible things by themselves with limited tools. But for many makers, the right tools can help an idea become reality. The opportunity to share information, help, and hang out with other makers is also useful. Often, makers can achieve more—and spend less money—when they share ideas, skills, tools, and supplies with each other. Different **perspectives** help them think in fresh, new ways. That's the idea behind makerspaces. If this sounds fun or interesting to you, then you're a maker who might work well in a community makerspace. Makers need space, tools, information, and community. Makerspaces are where all of these people and things come together in one place.

Invention Happens Anywhere!

Steve Jobs and Steve Wozniak were the founders of the Apple computer company. They made some of the first Apple computers in Jobs's parents' garage. It may have seemed like a small, unimportant makerspace at the time. Even though it was just a regular garage, Jobs and Wozniak used it to make one of the first personal computers!

Chapter 2

What Are Makerspaces?

T he word *makerspace* is a general term for a place where people get together to make things. Makerspaces might focus on electronics, robotics, woodworking, sewing, laser cutting, computer **programming**, or some combination of these skills. In

At makerspaces, makers help each other solve problems by brainstorming, trial and error, and hard work.

fact, really cool things happen when makers combine materials and ideas from different kinds of skills and tools. The kinds of tools found in makerspaces reflect the interests of the community.

Members of makerspaces might be beginners who make stuff for fun or professionals who use the space as an office. They might be small business owners who are testing out ideas that they hope will improve the world or earn them money. You might join a makerspace community by chipping in to buy tools that other members can use. Like a gym membership, you might buy a daily, monthly, or annual pass. Sometimes, you will find makerspaces in libraries, church basements, and community centers. Some classes and activities might even be free!

What Might You Find in a Makerspace?

No two makerspaces are the same, but here are some tools that makerspaces might have:

- laser engraver
- 3D printer
- sewing machines
- **soldering** irons
- woodworking tools
- metalworking tools

Maker communities are popping up around the world in small towns and large cities. They are places where people come together to learn, plan, and create. They are stocked with many kinds of tools and supplies. Members of makerspaces know that they are joining a community. They know that they aren't there to show off but to use what they know to help others. In return, their fellow members might teach them something new. Some larger makerspaces have full-time staff members who can fix broken machines, teach people how to use tools, and give other help as needed. Makerspaces often partner with other businesses, libraries, or organizations to offer classes on topics like sewing, computer programming, or cooking.

Some makerspaces are equipped with expensive power tools. Sometimes, these tools are computer controlled for precise movement. A makerspace can be located anywhere from a garage in a backyard to an office building downtown. Some spaces are in huge warehouses with plenty of room to work on really big projects. Others are tiny spaces carved out in makers' homes.

Many makerspaces focus on STEAM subjects. *STEAM* stands for "science, technology, engineering, art, and math." Makers work with these subjects to come up with solutions to problems. For example, a scientist might partner with an **engineer** to design a new kind of plant-watering system. To design a program that can guess the probability of different things happening, a computer programmer might partner with someone who loves math. An artist might want to design a sculpture that uses a computer to control a series of light patterns. Some makerspaces specialize in one or all of the STEAM subjects.

You'll also hear people talk about hackerspaces. These are also makerspaces. Hacking is a term used for exploring and creating with technology. You may have heard the word *hackers* used to describe people who access computer systems illegally, but that's a different type of hacking. Most hacking is perfectly

Fab Labs

A fab lab is a special kind of makerspace that buys tools and equipment that are identical to those in every other fab lab. That way, when people travel to different cities, they are familiar with the equipment in the new makerspace.

You never know what kinds of projects you'll find in progress at a makerspace.

legal. Today a "hack" or "hacking" is a term used to describe any quick, functional fix to a problem or a need, such as using a book to prop up a computer.

Makerspace communities believe in the power of open-source creation. That means that when someone creates a robot, a piece of furniture, or a cool game, they share their plans, construction details, and computer **code** with the world. They are saying, "Here are my ideas. You are welcome to use them, change them, or make them better. Just share your changes with the world!" Using these ideas is not copying because an open-source creator has given you permission in advance. When something is open source, the author shares it with others who can use it in new ways.

Power tools and computers may be inventions of the last hundred years, but communities have been making stuff since the beginning of human history. Think back to your history classes. Hundreds of years ago, makers such as painters or blacksmiths had professional clubs called **guilds**. Guild members trained students and challenged one another to do great work. Today, pottery guilds are clubs where **amateur** or full-time clay artists come together to make pots, plates, and decorative items. Quilt guilds and quilting bees have existed for hundreds of years. Today, it is not only people with the same skills who work together. People with a variety of skills come together to share perspectives, experience, and tools. Where might people in your town gather to share stories or teach skills? Could it be a makerspace?

Chapter 3

Makerspaces in Real Life

Do you want to design Web sites and make **software**? You might like to travel to Berlin, Germany, to visit c-base. It was founded in the 1990s as a place for people to develop skills in computer software, **hardware**, and **networks**. It's considered one of the first hackerspaces in the world. Today, c-base supports hundreds of musicians, artists, robot designers, and many other makers in Berlin. It is a nonprofit organization. This means that its main purpose is not to make money. It is funded by members and donations.

Would you rather stay in the United States and learn about robots? Take a trip to Dallas, Texas, where members of the Dallas Personal Robotics Group get together to share ideas for making robots. Is making art more your style? Travel to Saratoga Springs in

C-base sometimes hosts events where makers can listen to experts dicuss the latest technology.

upstate New York to see Yaddo, a famous artist's community that was formed over a hundred years ago. It's a place where painters, filmmakers, and just about any other type of artist you can think of gather together to make and create in a welcoming environment.

Some communities, such as Ann Arbor, Michigan, have several hackerspaces and makerspaces. Ann Arbor's University of Michigan campus offers spaces and resources for faculty, staff, and students. Other people can learn programming at All Hands Active, carve wood at Maker Works, and program microcontrollers at the Ann Arbor District Library. Some makerspaces are based permanently in specific buildings. Others are short-term pop-up spaces that are only used for a few days or a few weeks before shutting down.

Students at this Plymouth, Michigan, maker group learned how to program computers.

No matter what is being made in these spaces, the idea is that two minds (or three or four or eight) are better than one. People can buy better equipment and more workspace when they share the cost. When people partner with one another to create projects, they can pool their expertise and accomplish more. That is mostly what community makerspaces are about—connecting with people, making friends, and working with one another to improve ideas.

Find a Makerspace!

Do you want to get involved in a makerspace? Here are some ideas for how to find one:

1. Look in your local yellow pages or do an online search for the name of your town or closest city and the words *makerspace, hackerspace, workshop, guild, hobby group, hobbyists, or club.*

2. Ask your teachers if they know anyone who makes the type of things you're interested in learning how to make.

3. Librarians are very good at helping people find information, so don't be afraid to visit your library's help station or reference desk. That's what they're there for!

4. Contact the arts or engineering departments at local colleges and universities.

5. Keep an eye out for hobbyist or maker activities in the community calendar or events section of your local newspaper. Many makers like to get together to show what they've made. They're also happy to connect you with other makers.

Makers can do almost anything when they put their minds together.

Chapter 4

Visiting a Makerspace

Some makerspaces are equipped with computers for programming, editing video footage, or anything else makers can imagine.

There are many different types of maker-spaces. Some are like being at school. They are organized and quiet. Others are full of loud machines and power tools that take up a lot of space. Many makerspaces are filled with people working together in teams, improving their projects by working together.

The first thing you need to know is when the space is open. A makerspace in a library might be open just a few hours a week when groups meet. A membership makerspace might be open many hours a day in its own building. Others might meet once a month at a mall or library meeting space. Call and ask if you can visit and get a tour. Ask about the kinds of activities that go on there. Find out what kinds of activities are open to kids and teens.

When you get there, take a look around, and don't be afraid to ask questions. Makers love to answer questions! If people are not friendly to you, then it's not your kind of space.

Makerspaces have lots of different tools in them, because each tool fits a different need. If you want to sew a blanket or a pillow, you will need a sewing machine. If you want to build a wooden bench, you will need a hammer, nails, and maybe even power tools. Each space offers different tools to fit its members' needs. You might see saws to cut wood or plastic. Drill presses can make holes in things. High-temperature soldering irons help makers attach wires to electronic devices. 3D printers can turn a design on your computer into a plastic object. Ask what kind of training is required before you can use those tools. Are there classes that teach you, or will a member or staff member be available for one-on-one help? What is the class schedule? Is it free?

Also take a look at the workspace. If you want to bring your laptop, will it be safe from the sawdust of a drill press? Are there spaces where you can work quietly? What about places where meetings and classes are held? Are there places where you can store your project between work sessions? What kind of table space is there? Can you spread out your quilt? Will you have room to take apart your old VCR?

Keep an eye out for signs that safety is important to the community. Some of the tools in makerspaces can be dangerous. That's why training and classes are so important. Safety is one of the most important things for a successful makerspace. You can think of these makerspaces as labs for experiments and making dreams become reality. But all labs come

Many woodworking tools can be dangerous without the right protective equipment.

with guidelines to make sure everyone stays safe. It's important to remember that many projects involve cutting, hammering, needles, or even fire. Some tools can cut through and shape metals like aluminum or steel. You will probably need help from a trained adult to use these machines.

When you're working in a makerspace you can use the "three Gs" to keep you safe: goggles, gloves, and guidance. Why would you need to wear goggles? When you're cutting wood, metal, or plastic, little pieces can get into your eyes. You should wear goggles even if you're not cutting anything yourself. Someone else could be cutting these materials with a power tool nearby. When you're in a space with power tools or where cutting is happening, goggles will keep your eyes protected.

Gloves are useful for a lot of reasons. They improve your grip and allow you to handle things that are hot or have rough edges. They also protect against cuts, bruises, or scrapes. Remember to wear gloves if you're working with rough material or liquids that might damage your skin, like melted glue from a hot

Gloves can protect your hands from a variety of common dangers while you are working.

glue gun. Suede or cloth gloves protect your hands from splinters. Latex or plastic gloves protect your hands from paint or chemicals. Check the label to make sure you have the right glove for the job.

Guidance is one of the most important ingredients in the recipe for a good makerspace. It's important to remember that a lot of the activities that go on in a makerspace require an adult to supervise or help you. Many adults also need guidance and training when using makerspaces. People come to makerspaces because they want each other to be safe and get better at what they do. They don't want to see you fail or get hurt, so ask for help when you need it.

Name That G!

In the following situations, which should you use: gloves, guidance, or goggles?

1. You are making a rocking horse for your little sister. You have drawn the plans, but you need to cut the wood. A local carpenter named Greg has offered to cut the wood while you watch. What should Greg wear? What will you wear when you watch him?

2. Eva is taking a class in which she will learn to solder wires together. What should she do to stay safe in the class?

3. Fred is helping his grandmother make a quilt for his cousin's new baby. His grandmother knows how to assemble a quilt, but Fred wants to use the local quilt guild's sewing machine. What should he keep in mind?

Chapter 5

Inspiration

So far in this book, we've talked about a lot of tools and types of groups that are committed to making and hacking. How can you get inspired about what to make? How do you learn about new things you might be interested in? What would you be proud to make yourself?

Your local library is a terrific place to start when thinking about these questions. Ask your librarian to help you find books that include projects and magazines like *Family Handyman, MAKE, American Girl,* and *Boys' Life*. Browse the pages and look at examples of what other kids and families are making. Which projects look challenging but not too difficult for you to complete? Do you think you'd be happier making something out of fabric or something out of wood?

The Internet is another popular place for makers to swap ideas for projects. There are many online

You can go online to find plenty of great ideas for new projects.

communities where people freely share photos, sketches, tutorials, and directions for making their projects. Just be safe if you join a community. Avoid revealing personal details in your posts. YouTube is a great place to look for video lessons from other makers. We've listed some of our favorite sites on the next page.

Web Sites to Jump-Start Your Maker Imagination

www.makezine.com offers examples of projects, kits you can buy, special events, and more

www.instructables.com offers tutorials on how to make electronics, crafts, and more

www.adafruit.com provides information about robotics, electronics, and computer engineering

www.makeprojects.com is a great place to search for project ideas

www.sylviashow.com shows you how to make electronics, crafts, sewing projects, and more

www.scratch.mit.edu is a great source for beginner programming projects

www.howstuffworks.com explains how things work in plain, simple language

www.codeacademy.com and *www.khanacademy.com* can help you learn how to program software and create Web pages

www.webmaker.org can show you how Web pages are made

www.stencyl.com can help you practice your programming skills

Now that you know you're a maker and you have some ideas, go out and find a makerspace. Can't find one? Ask your teacher or librarian if you can start one at school. Have fun, and keep making!

What will you make at your makerspace?

Glossary

amateur (AM-uh-chur) a person who performs skills or activities nonprofessionally

code (KODE) text written in a computer programming language

engineer (en-juh-NIER) someone who is trained to design and build machines or large structures

guilds (GILDZ) groups or organizations of people who do the same kind of work or have the same interests

hardware (HAHRD-wair) computer equipment, such as a printer, monitor, or keyboard

networks (NET-wurks) groups of connected computers and other communications equipment

perspectives (pur-SPEK-tivz) particular attitudes or ways of looking at something

programming (PROH-gram-ing) the process of creating programs for computers

software (SAWFT-wair) computer programs

soldering (SAHD-ur-ing) the process of joining pieces of metal by putting a small amount of heated, melted metal between them

Find Out More

BOOKS

Ceceri, Kathy. *Robotics: Discover the Science and Technology of the Future with 20 Projects.* White River Junction, VT: Nomad, 2012.

Platt, Charles. *Make: Electronics.* Sebastopol, CA: O'Reilly, 2009.

Robertson, J. Craig, and Barbara Robertson. *The Kids' Building Workshop: 15 Woodworking Projects for Kids and Parents to Build Together.* North Adams, MA: Storey Kids, 2004.

WEB SITES

See the list in chapter 5!

Index

About the Authors

Samantha Roslund (left) is a school library media master's student at the University of Michigan in Ann Arbor and helped develop Michigan Makers, an afterschool makerspace for middle schoolers.

Emily Puckett Rodgers (right) is actively involved in makerspaces and hackerspaces in the Ann Arbor, Michigan, area when not working as a special projects librarian for the University of Michigan Library.